AFRICAN WILDLIFE

THEMES

DEDICATION

For Mom, Dad, Judith, Justin, Elizabeth and Alan.

AFRICAN WILDLIFE

THEMES

RICHARD DU TOIT

Struik Publishers

(a division of New Holland Publishing (South Africa) (Pty) Ltd)

Cornelis Struik House

80 McKenzie Street

Cape Town 8001

Website: **www.struik.co.za**

First published in 2001

1 3 5 7 9 10 8 6 4 2

Copyright © in text: Richard du Toit 2001

Copyright © in photographs: Richard du Toit 2001

Copyright © in published edition: Struik Publishers 2001

Publishing manager: Pippa Parker

Designer: Janice Evans

Editor: Helen de Villiers

Proofreader: Jeanne Hromnik

ISBN 1 86872 589 8

Reproduction by Hirt & Carter Cape (Pty) Ltd

Printed and bound by Sing Cheong Printing Company Limited, Hong Kong

ACKNOWLEDGEMENTS

Firstly I want to thank my friend Bobby Haas. Long may we journey together through Africa's wildernesses on photographic adventures!

Thanks to Gerald Hinde for his help and friendship over many years, and those legendary lunches!

And thanks to Molly Buchanan for her support over the past few years.

I want to thank Jonathan Gibson, Helge Haniger, Karl Parkinson, Concetta Serretta and Ronell Power of Chobe Game Lodge for ongoing help and support.

Thanks to Pippa Parker at Struik for initiating this book and steering it along to completion. Janice Evans deserves a special mention for all her creative ideas and for designing this book from scratch – thank you. Finally, thanks to Steve Connolly, Helen de Villiers and the rest of the talented Struik team – it was a pleasure working with all of you.

Half title: A grizzled male warthog sports impressive warts and a fine set of tusks. Sharp-eyed and alert, he will be the veteran survivor of many a lion attack.

Title spread: A gemsbok crests a dune.

Opposite: Although endangered in southern Africa, Wattled Cranes are still common in the Okavango Delta.

This page: Elephant bulls monopolize a small waterhole, preventing other creatures from coming to drink. It is a hot, dry morning and the summer rains are still to arrive.

Overleaf: Red-billed Quelea flutter at dusk, their tightly bunched flight creating an ornate pattern.

contents

author's introduction

The great, untamed continent of Africa is home to a wonderful diversity of creatures and plants. Here in southern Africa we have access to an almost unparalleled array of wildlife reserves, national parks and other wilderness areas. These wild places, ranging from densely vegetated tropical bush, through savanna grassland, to stark, arid stretches of desert, offer opportunities, challenges and rewards to anyone with a spirit of adventure.

Over the past few years I have travelled throughout southern Africa in pursuit of images of wildlife and nature. My journeys have taken me to many of the wilderness areas and national parks in South Africa, Botswana, Zimbabwe and Namibia. The beauty, abundance and diversity of wildlife across the region is staggering, and there is no other place in the world where I feel more at peace.

Nature provides one with an infinite variety of events and extraordinary moments to observe and try and capture on film. Even after 10 years of photographing wildlife, I continually witness new and unusual things. The recurring cycles of drought and regeneration, and the daily life and death dramas played out against this beautiful backdrop, are at once disturbing and captivating. For its peaceful timelessness, as well as its natural theatre, people fall in love with the African bushveld, and return again and again.

Many other wildlife books concentrate on specific animals or regions of southern Africa. When I catalogue my slides I also group them in such a way. However, in order to look at things from a different perspective in this book, we decided to group our selection of images into seven distinct themes: Up close, In action, Going solo, Pairs, Families, Neighbours and Moods. In this way we have covered a wide range of subjects that depict the beauty and wonder of nature throughout our region.

All of the animals and plants in this book were photographed under natural conditions. None of the subjects were interfered with in any way; they weren't captured, chased, or attracted with food or calling. All the animals were wild and free, living in their natural habitat.

In this day and age computers can be used to modify images extensively. These changes are often undetectable, and can significantly distort the reality of the image. None of the photographs in this book have been manipulated or altered in any way. Every photograph is a true and accurate record of the behaviour of animals and natural occurrences as seen through my camera lenses, and captured on film. To ensure a fresh approach, only images that have not been previously published in other books were selected.

Nearly all the animal photographs in this book were taken from my vehicle. A vehicle functions well as a portable hide that provides safety when one is close to large animals, and ensures that smaller ones do not flee the area.

For this project I used two zoom lenses, the 17 - 35 mm f2.8 and the 70 - 200 mm f2.8, and I also made use of a 500 mm f4.5 fixed lens. All the photographs were shot on ISO 50 and ISO 100 slide film.

I hope you enjoy paging through this book as much as I have enjoyed photographing Africa's wildlife.

Richard du Toit.

The tracks of seed-searching turtledoves weave patterns on the Kalahari sands. It is early morning and soon the winds will dissolve these ephemeral footprints. By midday, with the rise in temperature, the grains of silicon will become too hot for bird or beast to walk on.

up close

The silvery dewdrops that decorate spiderwebs at dawn reveal hundreds of webs in every tree and plant. Golden-orb web spiders (opposite & top right) spin huge, sticky webs that are strong enough to catch the largest of insects and even small birds.

Fresh blades of grass sprout from the trunk of a Mopani tree felled by elephants. In nature, nothing goes to waste.

Clusters of fallen round-leafed teak flowers are held in the tight embrace of spring grasses.

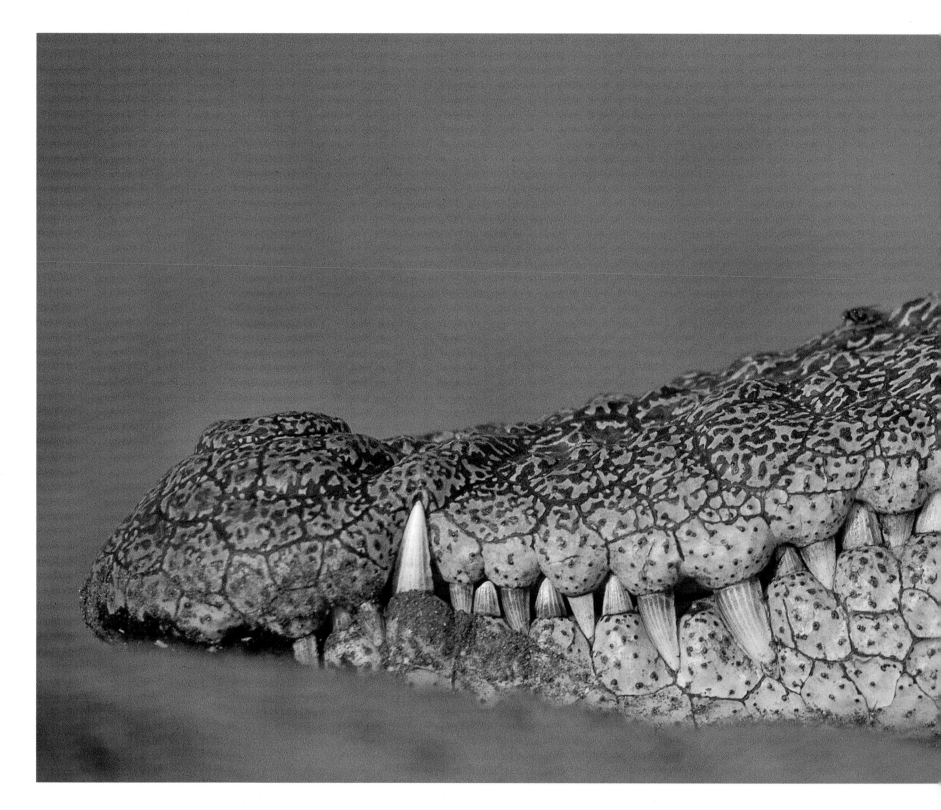

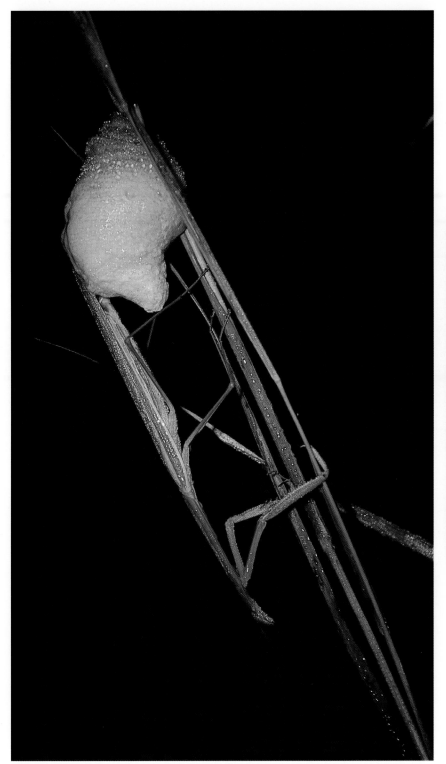

Previous pages: The gently smiling jaws of a Nile crocodile. The local colloquialism 'flat-dog' stems more from respect than affection for these feared reptiles.

Little creatures abound: a painted reed frog (opposite) clings to a lala palm. In summer, these tiny frogs appear in a wide variety of colours. In the cool hours before dawn a female praying mantid lays her eggs in an egg case that she has attached to a grass stem (left). A long-horned katydid (above) blends cryptically into a succulent flower.

Being in close proximity to relaxed elephants is an enthralling experience. Should you have the good fortune to look closely into the eye of an elephant, you will recognize a kindred spirit, and know instantly that they too have souls.

Winter waterholes are visited on a daily basis by elephants. The antics and activities of these magnificent beasts provide an endless source of fascination for observers. The elephant's extraordinary trunk must surely be the most versatile organ in the animal kingdom.

The scents and colours of flowers advertise a rich supply of sweet nectar, attracting myriad insects. These abundant, feasting creatures, in turn, attract the attention of insect-eating hunters. A Natal green snake (opposite, left) streams effortlessly upwards from a flowering aloe. By resembling a sprig of fallen leaves swaying in the breeze, a slow-moving chameleon remains unnoticed by enemies as it inches to safety (opposite, top right). A male Scarlet-chested Sunbird (opposite, bottom right) sips nectar. He will also feed on insects. The caterpillars of the African monarch butterfly (above) feed on the toxic milkweed plant, which renders them unpalatable as prey. Here, the adults use their long proboscises to reach the nectar.

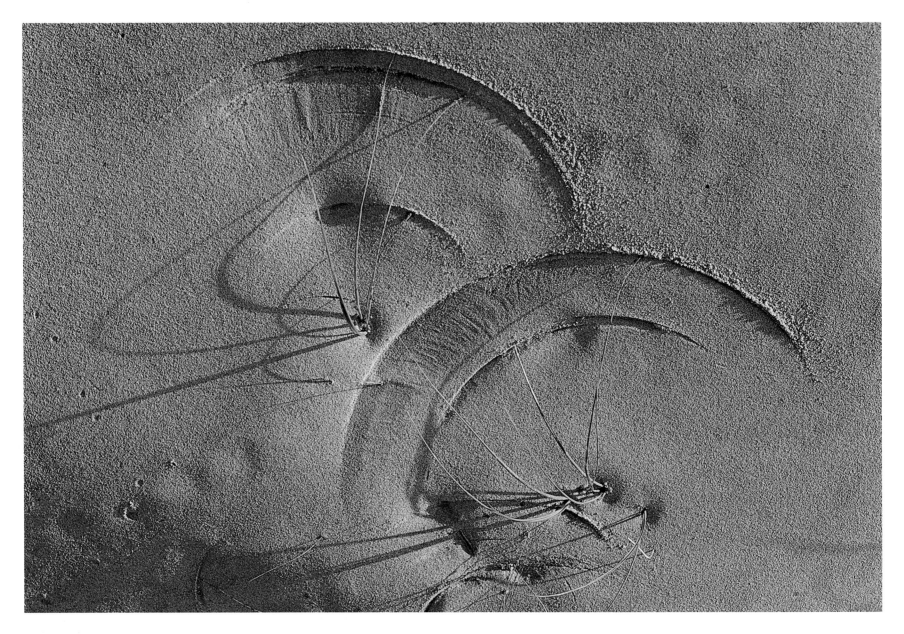

For plants, a sandy beach is a challenging and unstable environment. Winds whip the grasses to create circles in the hard sand.

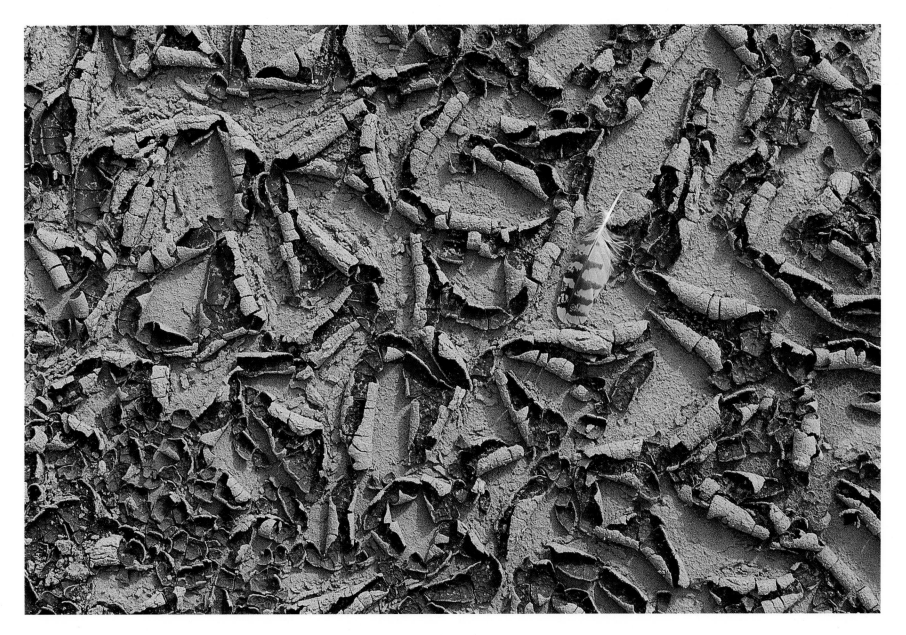

During the night, the first rains of summer have left shallow puddles. In the scorching heat of day they will dry and vanish within hours, cracking and curling a brittle layer of mud.

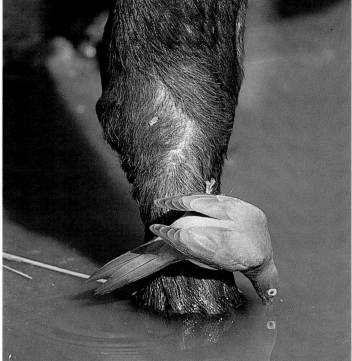

The buffalo is a favourite multi-purpose host of the Red-billed Oxpecker. Propping themselves up with stiff tails and clinging with curled claws, oxpeckers groom buffalo fur for invertebrate snacks. The huge bovids also serve as convenient perches for sipping water, as well as drying out, preening and resting after a bath in the river.

Young cheetahs chase each other in mock hunts in the half-light of dawn. The skills learnt during play will stand them in good stead as they approach that difficult and dangerous stage – the beginning of independence.

in action

Kudus take fright as they approach a summer waterhole (opposite). The cause of their panic is a hyaena, asleep in the water, that has woken and suddenly lifted its head. Zebra stallions (above) joust and feud as family groups meet up at a waterhole. Thrashing hooves and sharp teeth are the weapons in these sudden battles, but serious injury is seldom inflicted.

Overleaf: In Botswana, young elephants often fall victim to large lion prides.
Their small size and growing independence make them vulnerable.

In a titanic river battle, bull hippos fight over the right to mate with a cow. Battling on for several hours, they splash and chase each other up the narrow river, uttering guttural grunts and roars. Nile crocodiles are generally lethargic, but they are capable of surprising speed. This old individual (opposite) is snatching catfish out of a river rapid.

In the low light of dawn there is a fresh crispness in the still air. The clear sounds of night creatures merge with the
dawn chorus of birds. But the pace of life does not let up – all around there is a quiet urgency.

Even the thick skin of an elephant can be pierced by the proboscis of some biting flies. Mud baths are a favourite activity, both to protect and cool the giant pachyderms.

Hippo bulls squabble in a steadily drying pool in the Okavango Delta. Serious fights are rare; a far safer strategy is to posture and advertise your strength, and thereby avoid getting into potentially dangerous confrontations.

Raptors are the masters of the sky. Equipped with broad wings, they soar high on thermals, from which vantage point they search for victims.
Martial Eagles guard their nest (above); a Fish Eagle floats on a strong wind (top right); and a Secretary Bird runs before take off (bottom right).

The hooded eyes of raptors provide acute eyesight that is legendary. The hooked beaks and scimitar claws of these muscular birds are a deadly threat to most other birds and small animals. A Tawny Eagle alights on a branch (top, left); a Black Harrier hovers watchfully (bottom, left); and a Black Eagle lands at a cliff-face nest (below).

Many animals approach a waterhole with great caution. However, warthogs are the exception – they trot down quickly, but can dash away like a rocket. There are many dangers; lions, in particular, are most partial to these tasty morsels.

The untamed continent of Africa is home to a stunning variety of birds. Summer offers even greater variety, when migrants arrive and seasonal breeding plumages dazzle. Some of the regulars are the Yellow-billed Hornbill (opposite, top); the Lilac-breasted Roller (opposite, bottom); the Swallow-tailed Bee-eater (left); and the Reed Cormorant (below).

Lots of spots! Hunting in the warm winter sunshine, a young female leopard closes in on mice in the tall grass. While older leopards choose a more energy-efficient option by targeting larger beasts, this exuberant youngster breaks all the rules.

Saddle-billed Storks are endemic to Africa. Here a female Saddle-bill stabs for fish in a shallow stretch of river. Topped with a large yellow saddle, the huge upturned bill has serrated edges to help grip slippery victims. These are swallowed down in a single gulp; a belly full of wriggling fish makes for a satisfying morning's work.

Overleaf: In a manic feeding frenzy, crocodiles roll and fight over the remains of a carcass.

A male tree agama proudly advertises his spectacular appearance in the hope of attracting nearby females.
The use of resplendent colours is a common strategy in reptiles and birds – he will not go unnoticed.

going solo

A young male lion (opposite) rests at dawn after an active night. The hunt is a never-ending duel between predator and prey. The black-backed jackal (above) is widely distributed throughout southern Africa, but is likely to be seen only in protected areas.

A young giraffe strips leaves from a branch tip; Acacia trees are a favourite part of the giraffe diet. It is worthwhile taking the time to feel the sharpness of the thorns that protect these plants. It will leave you amazed as to how giraffes manage to eat them without ripping their mouths to pieces.

The rutting season comes at the end of summer. During April, male impala (opposite) become super-charged with testosterone. Their necks thicken, and the roars and grunts of these antelope echo through the bushveld, day and night. Both impala and springbok (above) rams horn vegetation at this time of year, the results of which can be curious adornments that they carry around for a while.

This may be the first time this immature Pale Chanting Goshawk
has seen water. Instinct plays a role in all animals' lives,
but the skills learnt by trial and error ultimately determine whether
he will live to adulthood and raise youngsters of his own.

After good summer rains there is an endless supply of food for the herbivores. A tree squirrel collects grass seeds (opposite, left); a young baboon daydreams while chewing on a stalk (opposite, right); and an impala ewe eats flowers (above).

A bontebok ram stands in fynbos in the early morning mists of spring. Bontebok are endemic to the southern tip of Africa, and the species has survived a close brush with extinction.

Steenbok are among the most widespread and successful of the antelope species. These tiny loners can survive without ever drinking water, for they obtain all their water requirements from the food they eat. Juicy blooms are munched with relish.

On a hot summer morning an energetic dung beetle rolls away elephant dung at a frenetic pace.
Nearby, in soils softened by recent rains, the ball is buried.

His face plastered with fresh mud, a solitary blue wildebeest bull offers up a bristly stare. Muddy faces and horns in male antelope result from ground horning, when they rub their facial glands on the ground.

After a night in their underground burrow, a pair of ground squirrels
emerge to stretch and sunbathe in the weak winter sunlight.

pairs

Blood brothers, these two lions are part of a coalition of four huge males that have dominated a stretch of the Khwai River in Botswana for many years.

Bull elephants graze on lush summer grass in Savute, Botswana. These relaxed elephant bulls remain here all year round, and in winter target trees for food.

A white rhino calf discovers his mother can be a useful scratching post. These behemoths produce a surprising variety of noises, with a vocal range of snorts and bellows through to high-pitched squeals.

Buffalo bulls (above) square up for some playful head bashing. The huge corrugated boss of horn is marked
red from scratching their heads on the bark of nearby trees.

Overleaf: Eastern Red-footed Kestrels, also known as Amur Falcons, are common summer migrants
from the northern hemisphere, arriving in flocks of hundreds of birds. Here, two males take a rest
from aerial forays in pursuit of insects.

Two young lion brothers slumber dreamily in warm winter sunlight. In the coming months they will leave the pride, and the strength of their bond will be vital in their quest for independence and survival.

Many birds form pair bonds that last for life. But here the association lies in the pursuit of
food. White-fronted Bee-eaters remove insect wings before swallowing their prey (opposite,
top). Yellow-billed Storks feel for fishes (opposite, bottom). And Carmine Bee-eaters (above)
watch from a fire-blackened stump for winged insects.

A Red-knobbed Coot feeds her tiny chick with algae she has collected from the pond floor.
Many baby birds have bright red beaks that stimulate their parents to feed them.

families

These cheetah cubs (opposite) are just three months old and still very vulnerable. A grassy mound provides them with elevation to
watch for both prey and enemies – in particular, the most ruthless predator of all, the lion. A young banded mongoose (above)
on one of his first foraging trips, accompanied by a babysitter. He has entered a bewildering and terrifying new world,
but the supply of food and constant chatter of other troop members provide comfort.

Overleaf: Elephant mothers form very close, lifelong relationships with their daughters. Cows
often stay with the herd for life, but young bulls leave as teenagers and wander off to new lands.

Baby warthogs are born in early summer, and leave their burrows to begin grazing when they are just over a week old (opposite).
An adult hippo indulges in a bit of playful threat-yawning with a youngster (above).

In primates, facial expressions are vital in communicating a host of messages. As a young baboon rides jockey on his mother's back, he practises threat yawns and staring techniques he will use all his life.

Black-backed jackals are monogamous, and raise litters of up to five pups that are born in late winter. In this way, their upbringing coincides with the early spring rains and consequent abundance of small mammals and insects that constitute their principal food.

A mother cheetah purrs as she enjoys the exuberant attention of her three-month-old cubs. It is the middle of the rainy season and the family is still wet from a passing thundershower. A litter of five youngsters is not unusual, but the mother will have to be continuously vigilant to keep them away from the major threat, the lion.

Many predators, from lion to mongoose, carry small infants in a similar manner.
A hyaena mother (opposite) carries her pups to a new burrow every week or so, whereas
the lioness (above) moves her babies around in a more haphazard way.

Overleaf: A pack of wild dogs and their young pups walk to a new den in an Acacia woodland. The adults know
the exact location of dens throughout their vast home range, where they can leave the pups while they go hunting.

A river bank is trampled flat by the daily traffic of thousands of grazers and other visitors needing a drink.
In summer, tall green grasses will sprout up, hiding the river until the return of the dry season.

neighbours

In winter, great flocks of Red-billed Quelea gather to drink (opposite and above). As a safety
measure, these birds maintain a very tight flock structure, flying so closely together that they appear
to be a single organism. Raptors risk serious injury by flying at speed into such a flock.
Two lionesses are startled by the sudden noise and passing shadows.

Overleaf: Giraffe and zebra group to drink. All around, the eyes of predators are watching. The green eyes of
crocodiles stare from the water, and in the fringe of the woodlands the amber eyes of lions take note.

Yellow-billed Storks rest and preen in the baking heat of a summer afternoon. Bull elephants stand monolithically in the shallows, occasionally slurping trunkfuls of water up out of their reflections.

Buffalo are the wild cattle of Africa. The ubiquitous cattle egrets accompany them to feast on the multitudes of insects flushed out by heavy feet.

Overleaf: A Carmine Bee-eater flutters as blue wildebeest march through the summer grasses of the Savute Marsh.
New calves born in the early morning will be running as strongly as their mothers even before they are one day old.

A bat-eared fox trots through winter grasses
silvered by the setting Kalahari sun.

moods

Thunder grumbles and lightning flickers from a distant Kalahari night storm. The rains have not fallen for nearly
a year and the fresh smell of summer rain will attract creatures from near and far.

For a few minutes before winter sunrise the hidden sun paints the sky a burnished golden red.
Now is the time for many of the smaller creatures to retire to their daytime hiding places.

On some days the harsh winter light is so bright it dazzles.
Silhouetted against the glare, ostriches crest a Kalahari dune (opposite, top);
and baboon and impala leap in the shallows (opposite, bottom).
A Cape mountain zebra is outlined by the cold winter morning light (below);
an elephant (right) drinks from the Zambezi River.

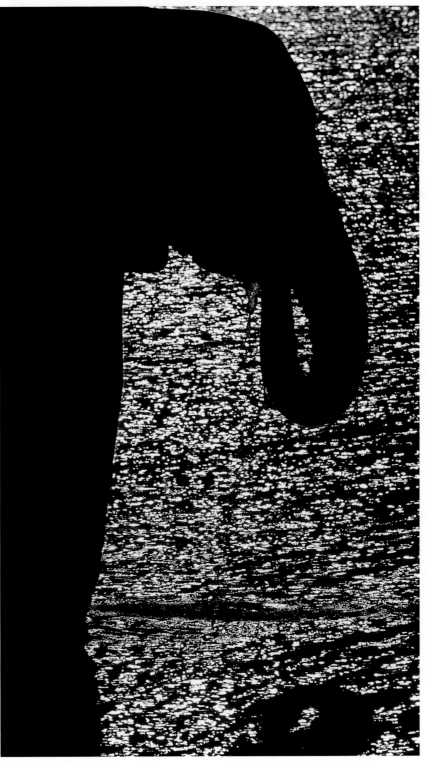

Songololo at sunset (above): when the hot desert sands have cooled, a millipede emerges from the depths of a squirrel burrow to forage on the dunes. On a carpet of trampled elephant dung (opposite), fragile mushrooms have appeared during the night. In the heat of day they will wither and die.

A Kalahari springbok (above) wanders across a dry thirstland where it may not rain for years.
An ostrich flicks cold stream water from its beak (opposite).

Fork-tailed Drongos are characters of the African bush. Here, one trails a herd of springbok in the Kalahari, snatching up flushed-out insects.

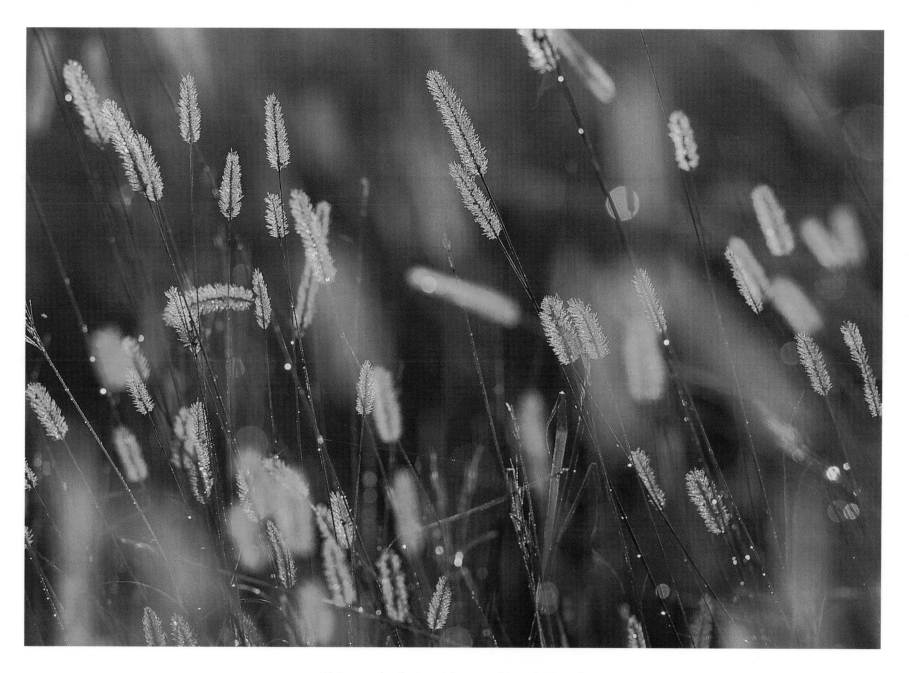

Winter grass heads glow at dawn on a Maputaland marsh.

Winter dust and smoke turn the lazy sun into a blood red orb. But the pulse of life does not
miss a beat: elephant, giraffe, impala and quelea all celebrate their freedom as another day draws to an end.

In the late afternoon, a female leopard patrols her territorial boundaries along a dry Kalahari riverbed.

A cheetah family stretches in the freezing dawn. During the night they did not move, instead huddling together for safety and warmth in a bundle of orange and black spots.

On a late afternoon in the dry season, elephant bulls daydream by the water.

The first rays of sunlight spill over red Kalahari dunes and into a dry riverbed.
A lioness passes by, and a herd of springbok trots nervously away.

The most magical time of day is before the dawn. It is a fleeting period of change when the smells, sounds and light combine in an indescribably beautiful and peaceful way.

The soft eastern glow warms a dark purple sky, and the stars slowly fade. A bull elephant marches past in the half-light of dawn.

A leopard's tail.
The end.